D1212723

The Berkeley, London

PRÊT-À-PORTEA

High-fashion cakes & cookies

Recipes created by The Berkeley's Head Pastry Chef
Mourad Khiat

Laurence King Publishing

Contents

Introduction

"The most exciting of English rituals that I adore is that of high afternoon tea. Even though I am not English, I love it, and always try to find some time to have a proper tea-time once in a while. You must respect it and indulge in the full ceremony of it."

Manolo Blahnik

My love of high fashion is perhaps predictable given my day job, but these days I'm as enamored by eating it as I am by wearing it, all thanks to the now legendary Prêt-à-Portea.

It's impossible not to rejoice in the beauty of a designer handbag made deliciously edible, as it is in the real thing; to be so smitten that there is little room for rationale or restraint. Allow me to carry you away for a heady afternoon of unrivaled glamor and exquisite taste in the form of miniature haute-couture cakes, cookies, and seasonal colored mousses served in shot glasses, all dreamed up by The Berkeley, pastry maestro Mourad Khiat, and his endlessly imaginative team.

Won't you join me in celebrating ten glorious years of my favorite high-fashion indulgence by recreating your own? Aprons optional, heels necessary, patience essential.

Erin O'Connor

About the recipes

"Fashion should always inspire creativity and fantasy, much like the feeling you get when you have that perfect dessert. You eat with your eyes first: presentation is just as important as taste."

Jason Wu

With Prêt-à-Portea—the first ever designer afternoon tea—a great deal of skill and passion goes into producing pastries that not only look super-stylish, but also taste exquisite, led by The Berkeley's Head Pastry Chef, Mourad Khiat.

Khiat was inspired to bake from a very young age by his father, who was also a baker and pastry chef. He enrolled in culinary school in Canada and worked his way up to become a leading pastry chef before moving to London. The Berkeley spotted his extraordinary talent and in 2006 he became the hotel's Head Pastry Chef. There, he and his team have skillfully crafted the stylish Prêt-à-Portea for more than a decade.

Each season Prêt-à-Portea showcases a different line-up of The Berkeley's favorite designers, inspired by the latest runway trends. This book features some of Khiat's most sought-after recipes, and shows you how to create your very own versions of these mouth-watering masterpieces.

Some are more complicated than others, but don't let that put you off! The level of baking skill required for each recipe is graded by heels: One heel for easy recipes; two for those that are a little trickier; and three for real challenges (but, much like super-high stilettos, they are absolutely worth it).

Top tips and techniques are explained at the back of the book, where you'll also find the templates you need to help you create your own designer cookies.

Have fun making these master pastry creations. And however it goes, you can always come and experience Prêt-à-Portea at The Berkeley and treat yourself to the original high-fashion afternoon tea by London's top cake couturiers.

FASHION RATING

Beginner   Intermediate   Advanced

JASON WU

———

The Catwalk Coconut
Cherry Compote

*" From the catwalk to an
elegant shot glass topped with
a tangy cherry compote, this sweet
is high glamor, complete with a
cheeky high-kicking tuile leg! "*

MK

The Catwalk Coconut Cherry Compote ﹁﹁

Be pretty in pink and wow your guests with the sweet taste sensation of cherry and coconut with cancan legs to finish. Expect calls for an encore.

MAKES 15

You will need: kitchen thermometer / fifteen 2 fl oz (¼ cup) shot glasses blender / rolling pin / nonstick silicone mat / 2-inch-diameter cookie cutter / baking parchment / baking sheet / paper piping bag

Ingredients

2 extra large egg yolks

1 tablespoon plus 2 teaspoons superfine sugar

2 leaves of gelatin

scant ½ cup whole milk

1 cup whipping cream

scant 1 cup coconut cream

The Coconut Mousse

Mix the egg yolks and sugar in a heatproof bowl. Soak the gelatin.

Now put the milk and a scant ½ cup of the whipping cream into a pan and bring to simmering point, taking care not to let it boil. Carefully pour it on to the egg yolk and sugar mixture, stirring continuously. Once everything is mixed, pour it back into the pan and cook on very low heat; don't stop stirring. When the mixture thickens enough to coat the back of the spoon, that's your cue to add the drained gelatin and yes, stir until it has dissolved.

Take the pan off the heat and pour the mixture through a fine strainer into a bowl. Stir in the coconut cream and leave to cool by setting the bowl in a larger bowl or sink filled with ice water. Keep an eye on it, and allow it to cool to 85°F.

Whip the remaining whipping cream to soft peaks, then fold it into the cooled coconut mixture. Now it's ready to pour into your shot glasses. Fill them three-quarters full and place in the fridge to set for two hours. No time off for you, however, there is more to do…

Ingredients

7 oz pitted fresh cherries

½ cup minus 1 tablespoon stock syrup (see page 111)

½ cup minus 1 tablespoon whipping cream

The Cherry Compote

Put the cherries and stock syrup in a pan, bring to a boil and cook gently for 7–10 minutes, or until the cherries are soft. Set aside to cool for a few minutes, then whizz to a pink purée in a blender. Whip the cream to soft peaks, then think pink and fold in the cherry purée. When the coconut mousse has set fully, pour the cherry compote on top, filling to just below the rim.

The Skirt

Roll out the pink modeling chocolate to a slim fitting of about ⅛ inch on a nonstick silicone mat. Use a 2-inch-diameter cookie cutter to stamp out 15 circles. To create the pleat, pinch the center of each circle and in a click of your fingers, it forms a tulip-like shape. Et voilà. Now set them aside—egg boxes are handy for holding the skirts while you turn to the tuile cookies.

Ingredients

3½ oz pink modeling chocolate

The Tuile Leg

Preheat the oven to 350°F/325°F fan. Melt the butter. Sift the flour and confectioners' sugar together into a small mixing bowl, then add the egg whites and melted butter and mix well. Chill the bowl in the fridge for 20 minutes.

Ingredients

3½ tablespoons unsalted butter

heaping ⅓ cup all-purpose flour

heaping ⅓ cup confectioners' sugar

1½ egg whites

black food coloring paste

Save a small amount of the mixture for the heels, but first comes the leg. Prepare the leg stencil and lay it on a piece of baking parchment on a baking sheet. Using a small spatula or knife, spread a thin layer of tuile batter (just as though you're spreading butter on to bread) over the stencil.

Cancan legs stencil at the back of the book

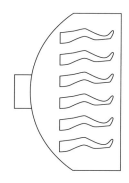

Take a deep breath, then gently peel away the stencil and your legs are ready for action! Repeat at least four times, which will give you 24 legs; they're super-delicate, so it's good to have a few extras in case of accidents such as leg or heel breaks.

To create the high heel, add some black food coloring paste to the tuile mixture you saved. You're going to pipe this on to the leg using a paper piping bag. First do the thin ankle strap, then the shoe itself, and lastly the heel. Stand by your oven and bake the cookies for just 2 minutes. Note: The cookies will be a pale shade when baked, but if they don't seem set after 2 minutes, blast for an additional 30 seconds. Watch them, though—even a trifle too long and they will burn.

Styling Details

Gently place a pink chocolate "skirt" upside down on top of a glass of mousse and cherry compote. Carefully balance the tuile leg in its center, or try making a little hole with a knife to help it stay steady—it's as tricky as it sounds. Hopefully it's kicking upwards. Repeat for the rest. Good luck!

ANYA HINDMARCH

—

The Blueberry Sponge
Handbag

"You see a bag—I see
blueberry sponge."

MK

The Blueberry Sponge Handbag ⌐⌐

Who says sponge can't get a seasonal makeover? This melt-in-your-mouth cake has the taste as well as the look of summer, as fruit and fashion color-coordinate with delicious results.

MAKES UP TO 24 (handbag size permitting)

You will need: plastic wrap (optional) / baking parchment / 8-inch square cake pan / stand mixer or hand-held electric beaters / wire rack palette knife / toothpick / paper piping bag

Ingredients

* Make a day in advance *

2 oz ready-to-roll icing

blue liquid food coloring
(or pick your favorite color)

The Handles

This finishing touch needs to be made the day before the cakes.

Place the ready-to-roll icing on a clean work surface, protecting it with plastic wrap if necessary, then add the food coloring to the icing and knead it in, spreading the color through evenly.

Once you have an even ball of blue icing the shade you want, take a small section and roll it under your hand into a cylinder as thin as you dare—think iPhone cable—then cut into 2-inch lengths. Bend each length into a neat, handle-like curve, with about 1¼ inches between the ends, and leave to dry overnight on baking parchment. Be sure to make at least 30, so that whatever happens, all cakes get a handle.

Ingredients

2¼ oz marzipan, cut into chunks

¾ stick unsalted butter, softened,
plus extra for greasing

½ cup superfine sugar

2 extra large eggs

¾ cup plus 2 tablespoons
all-purpose flour, sifted

a pinch of salt

1 teaspoon baking powder

7 oz blueberries

2 extra large egg whites

The Blueberry Sponge

Preheat the oven to 350°F/325°F fan. Grease an 8-inch square cake pan and line it with baking parchment.

Soften the marzipan, then put it in a bowl with the butter and ¼ cup of the sugar. Beat for 2–3 minutes, until pale and fluffy. Add the eggs, flour, salt, and baking powder; gently mix in the blueberries.

Whisk the egg whites with the remaining sugar in a grease-free bowl until soft peaks form, then fold into the blueberry mixture.

Pour into the prepared pan and bake for 20–25 minutes, until risen and golden. Leave to cool on a wire rack.

When cool to the touch, take the sponge out of the pan and cut it into rectangular pieces 1¼ x 2 inches (don't worry, there will be excess baggage). You could measure out a grid on a piece of baking parchment to guide your slices. Place each piece on the wire rack, standing up as in the image opposite, ready for its icing transformation.

The Icing

First place a sheet of baking parchment underneath your wire rack—it's going to get messy. If you want to cheat, you can buy ready-made icing, but if not, sift the icing mix into a large bowl. Add the water gradually, stirring gently, until the mixture is liquid but still thick, then add the food coloring and keep stirring. Once you're happy with the shade of your icing, gently pour or pipe it over your mini sponges so they are completely covered (except the bases), allowing the excess to drip on to the paper below. Leave to set for 1 hour.

Once the icing has set, gently remove each handbag from the rack with a palette knife and transfer to a serving plate. Take one of the icing handles and use a toothpick to mark two holes where it should sit on top of a bag. Either make a dent in the top of the icing, or add a dab of icing to "glue" on one fondant handle per bag and watch your sponge take shape.

Ingredients

2½ cups fondant icing mix

about 3 tablespoons water

blue liquid food coloring

Styling Details

To create the signature bow and any other fine detailing, make royal icing by mixing the confectioners' sugar with a little egg white and food coloring until it is about the consistency of lip gloss and the shade you want. When your hand is steady, put it in a piping bag, snip off the end to make a small hole, and pipe on the bow and other details.

Ingredients

½ cup confectioners' sugar

1 egg white

blue liquid food coloring

a steady hand

LANVIN

The Draped Honeycomb
Toffee Delice

*" Make a statement with
almond sponge as this silk top
becomes honeycomb mousse with
a light meringue ruffle to mirror
the soft shoulder drape. "*

MK

The Draped Honeycomb Toffee Delice ⌐

Indulge with these little French delights that will transport you to the creative home of haute couture as fashion and patisserie elegantly combine.

MAKES 40–60 in very delicately sized slices

You will need: baking sheet / baking parchment / stand mixer or hand-held electric beaters / plastic piping bag and plain ⅜-inch-diameter nozzle / 12 x 8-inch cake pan / aluminum foil / 12 x 8-inch lipped baking sheet / sealable plastic bag / rolling pin

---

Ingredients

* Make in advance *

heaping ½ cup superfine sugar

2 extra large egg whites

2 drops yellow liquid food coloring

The Meringue

This is not a spontaneous creative moment—the meringues need to be made at least the day before.

Preheat the oven to 140°F/100°F fan and line a baking sheet with baking parchment.

Put ¼ cup of the superfine sugar, the egg whites, and the yellow food coloring in a grease-free bowl. Whisk to form a light foam, then gradually sprinkle in the remaining sugar and whisk until it forms stiff peaks.

Now it's your turn to be artistic—look at the picture opposite. Fit a plastic piping bag with a plain, ⅜-inch-diameter nozzle and fill with the meringue mixture. Carefully pipe a ruffled leaf shape on to the lined baking sheet to echo the silk drape (you might want to do a few practice flourishes first). The finished cakes are only 2 inches long, so make sure your meringue leaves are the same, if not slightly smaller. Once you've filled a sheet with 50–60 ruffles, put the meringues in the oven to dry out for 3 hours. If your oven doesn't have a cool enough setting, don't worry; you can put them in at 200°F/175°F fan for 1 hour, or until dry. Remove from the oven and leave to cool completely on a wire rack, then store in an airtight container ready for the next stage.

The Almond Sponge

Preheat the oven to 400°F/350°F fan. Grease a 12 x 8-inch cake pan and line it with foil and baking parchment.

Tip: Use plenty of foil, pushing it tightly into the corners of the pan, to make sure the cake batter doesn't leak.

Melt the butter. Put the ground almonds, confectioners' sugar, flour, and whole eggs into a stand mixer or mixing bowl and beat for about 5 minutes, until pale and fluffy. Now add the melted butter and beat for another minute.

Put the egg whites in another, grease-free bowl, add the superfine sugar and whisk to form soft peaks. Fold it into the almond mixture and pour into the prepared pan. Bake for just 5–7 minutes, until golden and risen. Remove from the oven and leave to cool on a wire rack.

Ingredients

1 tablespoon unsalted butter, plus extra for greasing

¾ cup ground almonds

⅔ cup confectioners' sugar

2⅓ tablespoons all-purpose flour

2 extra large eggs

2 extra large egg whites

2½ teaspoons superfine sugar

The Chocolate Mousse

Pour the cream into a bowl and whip it to soft peaks, then set aside. Melt the chocolate, then remove from the heat and set aside.

Tip: Being organized is key in the kitchen. Lots of these recipes are complicated and done in stages, so "set aside" isn't a break, it's baking punctuation to help keep you on track!

Beat the eggs and egg yolks with the confectioners' sugar until light and fluffy. Fold the mixture into the chocolate, trying not to deflate the mixture too much, then stir in the whipped cream. Put it in the fridge to chill until needed.

Ingredients

2¼ cups whipping cream

10½ oz dark chocolate, broken into pieces

2 extra large eggs, plus two extra egg yolks

½ cup confectioners' sugar

The Honeycomb Toffee

You can easily buy honeycomb and skip this stage, but if you have time, make it yourself—it's fun to do.

Line a 12 x 8-inch lipped baking sheet with baking parchment. Put the golden syrup and sugar in a pan over low heat and cook until the mixture turns light brown. Add the baking soda and remove from the heat, but be careful—it will bubble and rise up in the pan. Stir it in gently. Pour into the prepared sheet, then leave for 30 minutes, until set.

Ingredients

3 tablespoons golden syrup

⅔ cup superfine sugar

4 tablespoons baking soda

The Honeycomb Toffee Mousse

Pour a scant ⅔ cup of the whipping cream into a bowl, whip to soft peaks, then set aside. Mix the honey and egg yolks in another large bowl and set aside. Soak the gelatin.

Pour the remaining cream into a pan with the milk and bring to a boil. As soon as it comes to boiling point, that's your cue to pour it on to the honey and yolk mixture, stirring continuously. Pour it all back into the pan. Add the drained gelatin to the pan, stirring until it has dissolved.

Simmer over low heat until the mixture is thick enough to coat the back of a spoon. Remove from the heat and strain through a fine strainer into a bowl to remove any egg residue. Think fashion and add the yellow food coloring to punch up the color, then cool it to 75°F in a large bowl or sink filled with ice water.

When it has cooled, gently fold in the whipped cream.

Now for the honeycomb toffee: pop a slab into a sealable plastic bag and crush with a rolling pin into bite-size pieces. Sprinkle the honeycomb toffee into the mousse mixture.

Ingredients

scant 1 cup whipping cream

scant ⅓ cup honey

2 extra large egg yolks

3 leaves of gelatin

6 tablespoons whole milk

2½ oz honeycomb toffee (made above!)

2 drops yellow liquid food coloring

Styling Details

It's all about layering. Spread the chocolate mousse evenly over the cooled sponge base and leave to set in the fridge for 1 hour. Once set, gently spread the honeycomb toffee mousse over the chocolate mousse and return to the fridge for another hour. After that pause, using a sharp knife, carefully cut the mousse and sponge layers into delicate rectangular slices measuring ¾ x 2 inches. Finally, place a meringue on top of each one and serve. Casual doesn't mean effortless, after all.

PHILIP TREACY

—

The Butterfly & Chocolate
Fascinator Dome

" *Showcase your icing and
styling skills with this chocolate
butterfly fascinator.* "

MK

The Butterfly & Chocolate Fascinator Dome ⌃⌃⌃

The skill of the original millinery inspired the complex glazing and icing techniques, but don't despair—the result is so delicious you'll wish for more!

MAKES 24—be generous with the butterflies

You will need: aluminum foil / rolling pin / butterfly cookie cutter, about 2 inches across / paper piping bags / kitchen thermometer / twenty-four 2-inch-diameter half-sphere silicone molds / wire rack

The Sugar Butterflies

Prepare and make the butterflies a day in advance.

First, fashion a few V-shaped molds from foil to rest your butterflies on while they set. Roll out each of the colored fondant icings to ¼ inch thick. Using a small butterfly-shaped cutter, cut out as many butterflies as you want to decorate your chocolate domes. Here we used about six per dome, but it's up to you how you cluster them. Once you have made enough butterflies in a selection of colors, place them gently in your V-shaped molds so that the wings don't set flat. Lift the edges to raise the wings into position (see image opposite) as you place them in the molds, and leave them with a sigh of relief to dry overnight.

To decorate the dried butterflies, mix the confectioners' sugar and egg white to make a paste the consistency of lip gloss (or you can take a shortcut by buying ready-made black and white icing). You will need two batches in two separate bowls. Leave one white, and add black food coloring to the other. Transfer each into a piping bag and decorate your butterflies.

The Chocolate Mousse

Mix the egg yolks with the sugar in a mixing bowl. Melt the milk and dark chocolates together and set aside to cool slightly. Soak the gelatin.

Pour the milk and ½ cup of the whipping cream into a pan and bring to a boil. Remove from the heat and add to the yolk and sugar mixture, stirring constantly. Once it is thoroughly mixed, pour it through a fine strainer to strain out any unwanted egg residue, and return it to the pan over low heat. Add the drained gelatin to the pan and stir until it has dissolved. Stir until the mixture is thick enough to coat the back of the spoon.

Ingredients

* Make a day in advance *

3½ oz each red, green, yellow, and purple ready-made fondant icing (or colors of your choice)

1 cup confectioners' sugar

1 extra large egg white

black liquid food coloring

Ingredients

3 extra large egg yolks

2 tablespoons superfine sugar

7 oz milk chocolate, broken into pieces

3½ oz dark chocolate, broken into pieces

2 leaves of gelatin

½ cup plus 2 teaspoons whole milk

1¼ cups whipping cream

Remove the pan from the heat, pour the mixture over the melted chocolate and leave to cool to 95°F. Whip the remaining cream and fold in. Pour the mixture into 2-inch-diameter half-sphere silicone molds, or a mini muffin pan lined with plastic wrap, and put it in the freezer to set for about 4 hours.

The Chocolate Miroir

Soak the gelatin (a chef's favorite secret ingredient).

Meanwhile—no time to rest—bring the sugar, glucose, and 4½ fl oz water to a boil in a pan, sift in the cocoa powder and stir well. Gradually pour in the heavy cream, stirring constantly. Add the drained gelatin to the pan and stir until it has dissolved. Pour it all into a pitcher and put it in the fridge to cool to 95°F.

Styling Details

Remove the mousses from the freezer and gently unmold each dome. Space them evenly on a wire rack set over a tray. Drum roll: now take the chocolate miroir mix out of the fridge and gently pour it over the mousses so that each is evenly covered, allowing the excess to run off on to the tray below.

Once the glaze is starting to set, which should be about 15 minutes, carefully slip a knife underneath each mousse and transfer it to a serving plate. Now to fashion up the dome. Place as many butterflies as you like on to each one to create your showpiece. Let the butterflies set into the miroir glaze as it dries. Beautiful. Now comes the best bit—taste one …

Ingredients

4 leaves of gelatin

1 cup superfine sugar

1 teaspoon liquid glucose

¾ cup cocoa powder

scant ¾ cup heavy cream

JIMMY CHOO

—

The Praline Pumps

" A slice becomes a pointed
pump when you add a
chocolate bow to finish. "

MK

The Praline Pumps ⤵

This easy yet irresistible praline slice is as essential to your baking repertoire as the perfect flat pump is to your wardrobe. This version combines rich texture with understated charm, and an excuse for gold glitter flakes.

MAKES 18—size and slice permitting

You will need: rolling pin / baking parchment / loose-bottomed 12-inch square cake pan / stand mixer or hand-held electric beaters / skewer kitchen thermometer / grater (optional)

The Bows

Although these are the finishing touch, you will need to make them a day in advance.

Ingredients

* Make a day in advance *

7 oz ready-made black fondant icing—easy!

Roll out the black fondant icing to ⅛ inch thick and cut it into ¼ inch x 2 inch strips. Fold both ends of each strip back so they meet in the middle to make a bow shape. Pinch the center of the bow together then wrap a smaller piece of icing around it to create the center point. Gently fluff out the bow to create wider loops and set aside on baking parchment to dry; if you're finding it fiddly, use a toothpick or even specialized marzipan tools (which you'll find in hobby stores). Cut and fold and fluff again, until you have at least 20 bows to allow for accidents or extra shoe slices.

The Sponge

Preheat the oven to 350°F/325°F fan. Grease a loose-bottomed 12-inch square cake pan and line with baking parchment. Sift the flour, cocoa powder, and baking powder together into a bowl. Melt the butter and chocolate separately, then set both aside to cool.

Ingredients

1½ cups all-purpose flour

¼ cup cocoa powder

1½ teaspoons baking powder

¾ stick unsalted butter, plus extra for greasing

2 oz dark chocolate, broken into pieces

5 extra large eggs

4½ tablespoons honey

scant ⅔ cup superfine sugar

½ cup whipping cream

Put the eggs, honey, and sugar in another bowl and whisk until pale and frothy. Fold the flour mixture into the egg mixture. Now stir in the cream and melted butter, and finally add that melted chocolate, stirring until the texture is smooth.

Pour the mixture into the prepared pan and bake for 15 minutes, until it has risen and a skewer inserted into the center comes out clean. Remove it from the oven and leave to cool.

The Praline Mousse

Soak the gelatin. Meanwhile mix the egg yolks and sugar together in a bowl. Put the milk in a pan and bring it to a boil, then slowly pour it on to the yolk and sugar mixture, stirring continuously. Carefully pour the mixture through a fine strainer and then return it to the pan. Over low heat, cook it gently, stirring, until the mixture thickens enough to coat the back of the spoon. Now is the time to add the chocolate spread to the pan. Continue to stir until it has dissolved completely.

Next, add the drained gelatin to the hot egg and milk mixture, stirring until it is completely dissolved. Allow to cool to 85°F.

Whip the cream to medium peaks, then fold into the praline mixture. Pour the mixture on to the cooled sponge base, spreading it out to cover the cake evenly. Now put it in the fridge and leave to set for 2 hours.

Ingredients

4 leaves of gelatin

3 extra large egg yolks

6½ tablespoons superfine sugar

⅔ cup plus 1 tablespoon milk

⅔ cup chocolate hazelnut spread (such as gianduja or Nutella)

1¾ cups whipping cream

edible glitter flakes or white chocolate, to decorate

Styling Details

Remove the cake from the fridge and cut it into strips 2 inches wide, then cut those into triangular slices about 2 inches long. Sprinkle with gold glitter flakes, or grate some white chocolate gently over the top of each pump. Take a black icing bow and place it near the point of the triangle to complete your pump. **Tip:** You'll find it hard to resist these comfy flats, but if you're not serving immediately, brush the underside of the bows with melted chocolate to stop the color from bleeding on to the praline.

AUTUMN/WINTER 2014

DOLCE & GABBANA

———

The Cassis Bavarois
& Chocolate Owl

*" Recreate an embroidered
woodland scene with a blue
chocolate owl and cassis base in
this make-believe bavarois. "*

MK

The Cassis Bavarois
& Chocolate Owl ᴧᴧ

As well as looking good, all our creations have to taste amazing, and this is a great example of how fashion, fun, and dessert skills combine.

MAKES 10
You will need: kitchen thermometer / ten 2 fl oz (¼ cup) shot glasses old plastic lid / baking parchment / paper piping bags / grater

The Cassis Bavarois

Ingredients

1½ egg yolks

1 tablespoon superfine sugar

1 leaf of gelatin

¼ cup milk

4½ fl oz whipping cream

½ cup cassis purée

15 drops blue liquid food coloring

Mix the egg yolks and sugar together in a bowl. Soak the gelatin. Put the milk and ¼ cup of the whipping cream in a pan and bring to a boil, then slowly pour it over the yolks and sugar in the bowl, stirring continuously. Strain the mixture through a strainer, then carefully pour it back into the pan. Using a kitchen thermometer, and checking and stirring as it thickens, cook very gently over low heat until the mixture reaches 185°F. It should be thick enough to coat the back of the spoon. Remove the pan from the heat.

Add the drained gelatin to the hot egg and milk mixture, stirring until it has dissolved. Now stir in the cassis purée and food coloring, and allow everything to cool to 85°F. The thermometer is key in this recipe.

Whip the remaining cream to medium peaks, then fold it into the cassis mixture. Ready? Now pour it straight into ten shot glasses, filling each glass so it's three-quarters full. Put them in the fridge to set for at least 4 hours.

The Panna Cotta

Ingredients

1 leaf of gelatin

3 tablespoons milk

¾ cup heavy cream

2½ teaspoons confectioners' sugar

1½ star anise pods

When the bavarois is set, soak the gelatin with the milk. Put the cream, confectioners' sugar, and star anise pods in a pan and bring to a simmer. Remove from the heat and leave it all to infuse for at least half an hour, then add the milk and gelatin, stirring well to dissolve the gelatin. Make sure the mixture has cooled to about 70°F, but not set—you need the wobble—before pouring it into the shot glasses as the top layer. (**Tip:** If the panna cotta sounds too complex, you can cheat and use whipped cream instead, but why not add the star anise for that touch of spice. Sshh!) Return the glasses to the fridge to set for 1 hour before you start on the next part.

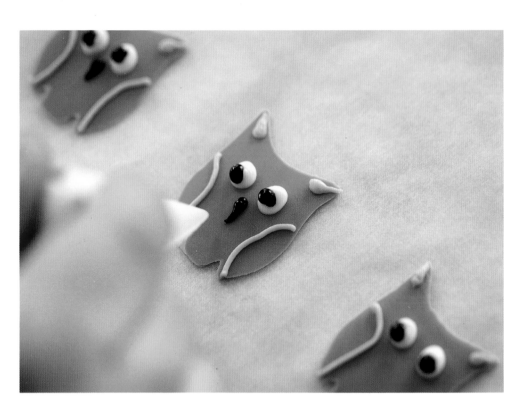

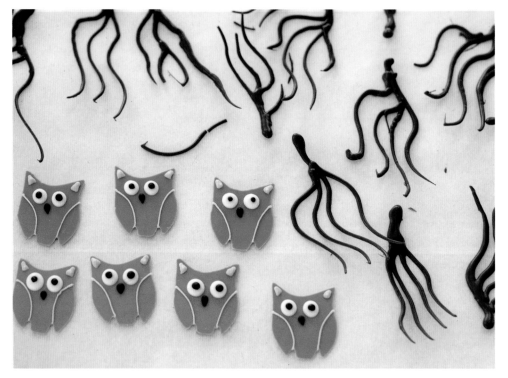

The Chocolate Owls

Prepare the owl template at the back of the book. Trace it on to a spare plastic lid and cut it out so that you have something to draw around.

Melt the white chocolate, being careful not to let it overheat. Add the blue food coloring—blue chocolate isn't a readily available thing, after all—and once all is combined, pour it on to a sheet of baking parchment, encouraging it to spread thinly and evenly. When it is partially set, use a small knife and the owl template to cut out ten bird shapes, plus one or two extras so that you can practice icing the details. Leave them to set completely, then carefully remove them from the parchment.

Styling Details

Save a little of the dark chocolate to grate over the panna cotta. Break the rest into pieces and melt, then put it in a paper piping bag and cut off the tip to create a small hole. Look at the image opposite—you need to pipe similar "branches" on to a sheet of parchment, creating at least ten in total. Include a thicker "trunk," which will help you to anchor the chocolate into the panna cotta. Leave to set.

To decorate the blue owls, prepare three paper piping bags (or you can buy ready-made icing pens, in which case you'll need one each in white, pink, and black). If you are making your own icing, start with the pink. Mix half the confectioners' sugar with a little water and a tiny drop of pink food coloring until you have icing the consistency of lip gloss. It's easiest if you pipe the pink ears and wing shapes first.

Mix the remaining confectioners' sugar with water as before, and put three spoonfuls into a paper piping bag. This will be the whites of the eyes, so pipe two on to each owl. While that dries, add a couple of drops of black coloring to the remaining icing in the bowl and again transfer to a paper piping bag. When the whites are dry, pipe small black dots on top of each one, trying not to make your owls cross-eyed, and finish with a black line below to make the beak. Give your owls some character as they strike a pose.

Finally, remove the shot glasses from the fridge. Grate shavings of the leftover chocolate over the panna cotta in the glasses to create your forest floor. Using the tip of a pair of scissors or a knife, clear a small space and press in an owl. Follow it with a chocolate branch, and your scene is set and ready to serve.

Ingredients

7 oz white chocolate, broken into pieces

⅛ oz blue liquid food coloring

Ingredients

3½ oz dark chocolate

½ cup confectioners' sugar

pink and black liquid food coloring

Chocolate owl template at the back of the book

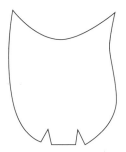

MOSCHINO

The Sugar & Chic Sponge Cake Bag

" Have fun with fondant icing and make a statement with a quilted bag in orange sponge. "

MK

The Sugar & Chic
Sponge Cake Bag ハハ

A handbag can not only have a sense of humor,
it can also taste delicious, if it's made from
orange sponge and wrapped in eye-catching
quilted red chocolate.

MAKES 24

You will need: rolling pin / 7-inch square cake pan / baking parchment
stand mixer or hand-held electric beaters / wire rack / paper piping bag

Ingredients

* Make a day in advance *

2 oz red ready-made
fondant icing

1 oz yellow ready-made
fondant icing

Ingredients

¾ cup plus 2 tablespoons
all-purpose flour

¼ teaspoon salt

1 teaspoon baking powder

¼ cup marzipan, cut into cubes

¾ stick softened unsalted butter,
plus extra for greasing

¼ cup superfine sugar

2 extra large eggs

3 tablespoons orange purée

½ extra large egg white

The Red Quilted Bag Cover

Make the bag handles and the quilted panels for the front of
your bags a day in advance, like a real artisan.

Roll slightly more than half of the red fondant icing to ¼ inch
thick, then use a knife to score it with straight diagonal lines
about ¼ inch apart (see photograph opposite, top right). Use a
ruler to keep your lines straight, and be careful not to press so
hard that you cut through the icing. Turn the icing by 90
degrees and repeat the scoring in the other direction, to create
a quilted effect. Cut the icing into 24 rectangles measuring
1½ x 1 inch and leave to dry in a cool place overnight.

Meanwhile, make the straps. Cut thin strips from the remaining
red and the yellow fondant icing and roll each into a thin
sausage. Take one of each color and twist them together to
create the bag's chain-effect handle, being careful not to twist
so tightly that the colors merge. Cut into 24 lengths of about
1¾ inches and fold into a U-shape. Leave these to dry in the
cool overnight as well.

The Cake

Preheat the oven to 350°F/325°F fan. Grease a 7-inch square
cake pan, and line with baking parchment.

Sift the flour, salt, and baking powder into a bowl, then gently
soften the marzipan. In a large mixing bowl, cream the butter,
2 tablespoons of the sugar and the marzipan until light and
fluffy. Lightly beat the whole eggs, then gradually beat them
into the butter mixture a little at a time. Fold in the sifted dry
ingredients, followed finally by the orange purée, and stir well.

In a separate, grease-free bowl, whisk the egg white to soft
peaks, then add the remaining 2 tablespoons sugar and whisk

again, this time to stiff peaks. Fold into the cake mixture. Carefully pour the mixture into the prepared cake pan and bake for 15–20 minutes. The cake is ready when it's risen and golden and a skewer inserted into the middle comes out clean. Leave to cool in the pan on a wire rack. Once cooled, remove the cake from the pan and, using a sharp serrated knife, cut it into 24 rectangles measuring 1½ x 1¼ inches.

Styling Details

Roll out the red modeling chocolate to ¼ inch thick. Using a sharp knife and the template, cut out 24 T-shaped pieces. Place a piece of orange sponge on the chocolate as shown in the photograph below, fold the short sides up, then wrap the remaining long end over to cover the cake completely. Press gently so the chocolate sticks to the cake and repeat for all the sponge pieces.

Place a small dot of melted white chocolate or icing in the center front of one handbag and stick on a quilted rectangle, as shown bottom right. Repeat for all the remaining bags. Put a dab of melted white chocolate or icing on each end of your woven handles and place one carefully on top of each cake. Repeat until all the handbags have a handle in place—it's not a clutch bag, after all.

For the ultimate finish, it's the attention to detail that sets these cakes apart. Sift the confectioners' sugar into a small bowl, stir in the egg white and yellow food coloring to make a paste, then put in a piping bag. (You could use a yellow icing pen instead, if you like.) Add a yellow border around the front of the bag and the M front and center, or your own initial if you are more inspired by your own branding.

Ingredients

7 oz red modeling chocolate

a little melted white chocolate or icing, for fixing

½ cup confectioners' sugar

1½ teaspoons egg white

5 drops yellow liquid food coloring

**Handbag template
at the back of the book**

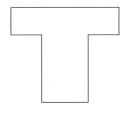

PAUL SMITH

—

The Raspberry & Mandarin Suit Mousse

*" Use zingy flavors
to capture this vibrant
suit in a shot glass. "*

MK

The Raspberry &
Mandarin Suit Mousse ⌐

*Fashion is about color and texture, and serving
up something both surprising and exciting—just
like these exotic shot glasses of summer fruits.*

MAKES 25
You will need: rolling pin / 1½-inch-diameter cookie cutter
twenty-five 2 fl oz (¼ cup) shot glasses

The Sugar Hats

Ingredients

* Make a day in advance *

3½ oz orange ready-made
fondant icing

Make these a day in advance so that they have time to dry. Roll
out the fondant icing to ¼ inch thick and use a 1½-inch cookie
cutter to cut out 25 neat circles. This is the brim of your bowler
hat, so make sure it is wide enough to sit on the rim of your shot
glasses. Next, bring the remaining fondant back together into a
ball, then roll it into a long sausage shape about ¾ inch in
diameter. Cut it into 25 slices about ¾ inches thick. Take one
slice, fashion it into a rounded dome to make the crown of your
bowler hat, and position it on one of the circle bases; it should
stick while the fondant is still soft. Repeat this mini millinery to
complete all 25 hats, then leave them in a safe place to dry.

The Mandarin Mousse

Ingredients

1½ extra large egg yolks

3¼ tablespoons sugar

1½ leaves of gelatin

⅓ cup whole milk

⅓ cup mandarin purée (or use
mango purée or orange juice)

7 fl oz whipping cream

17 drops orange liquid food
coloring

Mix the egg yolks and sugar in a heatproof bowl.
Soak the gelatin.

Put the milk in a pan and bring it to a boil, then, stirring
constantly, slowly pour it on to the egg yolk and sugar mixture.
Carefully pour everything back into the pan and cook gently,
over very low heat, still stirring continuously.

Once the mixture thickens enough to coat the back of the
spoon, add the drained gelatin to the hot mixture, stirring until
it has dissolved. Remove the pan from the heat, and pass the
mixture through a fine strainer into a mixing bowl. Stir in the
mandarin purée and the food coloring, then put the bowl in a
sink or large bowl of ice water and leave it to cool to 85°F.

Whip the cream to soft peaks, then fold it into the mandarin
mixture. Now you can pour the first layer straight into your shot
glasses, filling them one-quarter full, about an inch high (see the
picture opposite). Leave to set for 2 hours in the fridge.

The Raspberry Bavarois

When the mandarin layer is almost set, mix the egg yolks and sugar together in a heatproof bowl. Soak the gelatin.

Put the milk and a scant ¾ cup of the whipping cream into a pan and bring to a boil, then slowly pour it on to the yolk and sugar mixture, stirring continuously. Carefully pour the mixture back into the pan and stir while it cooks over very low heat. Once the mixture starts to thicken, it's time to add the drained gelatin to the hot mixture, stirring until it has dissolved. Remove the pan from the heat and pass the mixture through a fine strainer into a mixing bowl to extract any egg residue. Finally, stir in the raspberry purée and put the bowl in a sink or large bowl of ice water to cool to 85°F.

Whip the remaining cream to soft peaks, then carefully fold it into the raspberry mixture and pour it on top of the mandarin mousse, filling your shot glasses to the top. Once all are filled, put them in the fridge and leave to set for 2 hours.

Styling Details

Once all the hats are lined up and the mousses have set, remove the shot glasses from the fridge and finish their look with the striking orange hats.

Ingredients

2 extra large egg yolks

4 teaspoons superfine sugar

4 leaves of gelatin

scant ¾ cup whole milk

1⅛ cups whipping cream

scant 1 cup raspberry purée

VALENTINO

———

The Polka-Dot
Brownie

*" This is all about the polka dots!
Let them jump off the catwalk
and on to a delicious brownie. "*

MK

The Polka-Dot Brownie

A coat is a style staple of any wardrobe—just as a good brownie recipe can be your calling card. This is the best-dressed brownie ever, and comes with a bit of extra styling to wow your guests!

MAKES 28, but you can make more
You will need: 9-inch square cake pan / baking parchment / stand mixer or hand-held electric beaters / skewer / wire rack / rolling pin ¾-inch-diameter cookie cutter / plastic piping bag and plain nozzle

Ingredients

1¾ sticks unsalted butter, plus extra for greasing

9 oz dark chocolate, broken into pieces

3 extra large eggs

1⅛ cups light brown sugar

heaping ½ cup all-purpose flour, sifted

1 cup chopped walnuts

The Best-Dressed Brownie Ever

Preheat the oven to 350°F/325°F fan. Grease a 9-inch square cake pan and line with baking parchment.

Melt the butter and chocolate together and set aside to cool.

Whisk the eggs and sugar until pale and fluffy. Beat in the flour, followed by the melted chocolate and butter mixture. Fold in the chopped walnuts.

Now simply pour the mixture into the prepared cake pan and bake for 30 minutes. Patience is a virtue! When the time is nearly up, insert a skewer into the center of the cake; if it comes out clean, your brownie is ready. Remove it from the oven and leave the pan to cool on a wire rack.

Once cooled, remove the brownie from the pan. Using a serrated knife, trim off the edges and cut it into ten ¾ x 2-inch rectangles (draw this out on baking parchment if you want a grid to follow). Any excess is yours to eat—after all, it's important to taste what you're serving and styling.

Ingredients

3½ oz red modeling chocolate

scant 1 cup whipping cream

¼ cup superfine sugar

Styling Details

Roll out the modeling chocolate to ⅛ inch thick and stamp out about 20 circles using a ¾-inch-diameter cookie cutter. You want at least two per brownie, but you can use more, of course!

Now put the cream and sugar in a bowl and beat to medium-stiff peaks, taking care not to over-whisk it. Put this Chantilly mixture into a plastic piping bag fitted with a plain nozzle, and pipe small teardrops on top of the brownies, following the picture opposite. Position the red chocolate buttons between the teardrops of cream, and serve before you succumb to them all yourself.

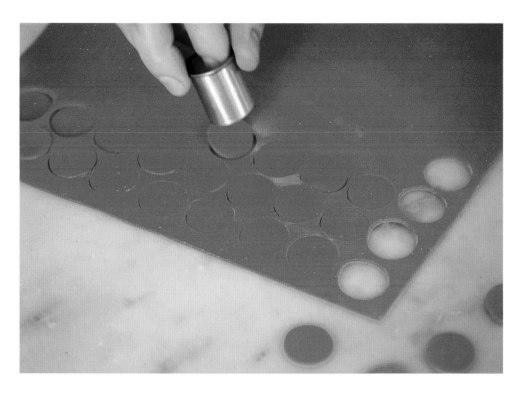

MULBERRY

———

The Rainbow Meringue
Summer Mousse

*"Imagine the English seaside
as you serve sunny lemon,
strawberry, and mint topped with
gorgeous pastel meringues."*

MK

The Rainbow Meringue Summer Mousse ꞈꞈ

This mousse is as irresistible as a sweet summer romance. Your friends will love it—dazzle them with a sunshine-filled rainbow of melt-in-your-mouth memories, served in a shot glass.

MAKES 25, but everyone will want more!

You will need: grater / blender / twenty-five 2 fl oz (¼ cup) shot glasses baking sheet / baking parchment / plastic piping bag and 2-inch star nozzle

The Lemon Curd Cream

Combine the lemon juice and lemon zest in a bowl. Beat the eggs and sugar together in a heatproof bowl, then place the bowl over a pan of simmering water, making sure it doesn't touch the water. Heat gently for about 3 minutes, whisking continuously, then add the lemon juice, zest, and butter, and continue to whisk until it thickens. Remove from the heat and strain your sunshine yellow cream through a fine strainer into a pitcher. Pour into 25 shot glasses to make the bottom layer. Leave to cool for 1 hour in the fridge. First of three done—but don't get too relaxed!

Ingredients

6 tablespoons lemon juice

finely grated zest of 2 lemons

2 extra large eggs

scant ¾ cup superfine sugar

1¼ sticks unsalted butter

The Strawberry Mousse

Now for the next layer. First, make a strawberry purée by whizzing the strawberries to a pulp in a blender, then treat yourself, add 1 tablespoon of the sugar, and stir to dissolve.

To make the mousse, mix the egg yolks and the remaining sugar in a bowl. Now put the milk and ¾ cup of the cream in a pan and bring to a boil, then pour it slowly on to the yolk and sugar mixture, stirring constantly. Once combined, carefully pour the mixture back into the pan and cook very gently, still stirring, over low heat until the mixture thickens just enough to coat the back of the spoon.

Soak and drain the gelatin, then add it to the hot egg and milk mixture and stir until dissolved. Now stir in the strawberry purée with the food coloring to intensify the shade. Allow to cool.

Finally, whip the remaining cream to medium peaks, and fold it into the strawberry mixture. Carefully pour it all into the shot glasses, on top of the lemon cream, to create the middle layer. Your glasses should now be two-thirds full. Return them to the fridge to set for 2 hours. This all takes time, but it's worth it!

Ingredients

21 oz strawberries

scant ¼ cup superfine sugar

3 extra large egg yolks

scant ¾ cup milk

1½ cups whipping cream

3 leaves of gelatin

30 drops red liquid food coloring

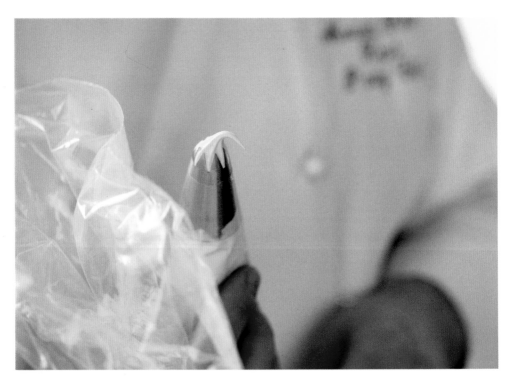

The White Chocolate and Crème de Menthe Mousse

Melt the chocolate and the butter separately and leave both to cool. Now whip the cream to soft peaks and set aside. Whisk the egg yolks and confectioners' sugar in a mixing bowl until pale and fluffy, then—that's right—set aside. (It's all about setting things up—just clear enough space for all these bowls.) Now pour the melted butter on to the chocolate, but do not stir at this stage. Soak and drain the gelatin, then put it in a heatproof bowl with the crème de menthe and microwave or heat briefly over simmering water until all the gelatin has dissolved.

Add the gelatin mixture to the chocolate and butter and stir gently. Pour this on to the yolk and sugar mixture, and stir so they combine thoroughly. Fold in the whipped cream immediately; the consistency will become nice and runny. Now carefully pour it into the shot glasses as the final layer. Return the mousses to the fridge until you're ready to assemble and serve.

Ingredients

5½ oz white chocolate, broken into pieces

¼ stick unsalted butter

scant 1 cup whipping cream

3 extra large egg yolks

3½ tablespoons confectioners' sugar

1 leaf of gelatin

scant 2 tablespoons green crème de menthe

The Meringue

Preheat the oven to 140°F/100°F fan and line a baking sheet with parchment. Whisk ¼ cup of the sugar with the egg white until soft peaks form, then gently sprinkle the rest of the sugar into the mixture, continuing to whisk. Once it rises in stiff peaks, divide the mixture into three separate bowls.

Now comes the fun part. Add the food coloring to each bowl, keeping each one a separate color. Fold the coloring very gently into the meringue so as not to deflate it. You'll create a slightly marbled effect. Fit a plastic piping bag with a ⅜-inch star nozzle and spoon each color of meringue carefully into the bag, so that as you pipe the colors combine to create a rainbow swirl. Pipe small swirls of meringue on to the prepared baking sheet and put the meringues in the oven to dry out for 3–4 hours. (It sounds ages, I know!) If your oven doesn't have a cool enough setting, put them in at 200°F/175°F fan for 1 hour, or until dry.

Once the meringues have dried out completely, carefully remove them from the baking sheet and leave to cool. Place one on top of each shot glass to complete your summer rainbow mousse.

Ingredients

½ cup superfine sugar

1 extra large egg white

5 drops each yellow, red, and green liquid food coloring

SIMONE ROCHA

———

The Floral Salted
Caramel Éclair

*" Delicate detailing to
inspire the chicest salted
caramel éclairs. "*

MK

The Floral Salted Caramel Éclair ᴧᴧ

Choux pastry is very much in fashion at the moment, so make this delicious twist on a favorite with sophisticated salted caramel cream filling and sugar flowers on top that is both naughty and nice.

MAKES 25

You will need: baking sheet / wire rack / stand mixer or hand-held electric beaters / plastic piping bags and plain ¾-inch nozzle / lipped baking sheet / plastic wrap / kitchen thermometer / skewer

The Éclairs

Preheat the oven to 400°F/350°F fan and grease a baking sheet ready for your choux pastry experience.

Put the milk and ½ cup water into a pan with the butter, salt, and sugar and bring to a boil. Remove the pan from the heat, then immediately add all the flour at once. Mix well, until the dough begins to come away from the side of the pan.

Transfer the dough to a stand mixer or mixing bowl and allow to cool slightly. Mix gently, adding the eggs gradually, one by one, until the mixture has a smooth, supple consistency. To check it, lift some of the mixture out of the bowl; if it flows back rippling like a cascading ribbon, then you have the right mix.

Put the mixture into a plastic piping bag fitted with a plain ¾ inch nozzle and pipe 25 straight lines 4 inches long in a row on the prepared baking sheet.

Bake for 25–30 minutes, until well risen and golden. Remove from the oven and leave to cool on a wire rack.

The Salted Caramel Pastry Cream

First line a lipped baking sheet with plastic wrap.

Mix the egg yolks, 5 teaspoons of the sugar, and the custard powder in a bowl and set aside.

Add the remaining sugar to 5 tablespoons water in a pan and bring to a boil, stirring occasionally to help dissolve the sugar. When it comes to a boil, stop stirring and let it simmer until it turns to a light brown caramel. Be very careful: if you leave it for even 30 seconds too long, the sugar will burn and be ruined, plus the smell is disgusting.

Ingredients

½ cup whole milk

1 stick minus 1 tablespoon unsalted butter, plus extra for greasing

heaping ½ teaspoon salt

1¼ teaspoons superfine sugar

scant 1¼ cups strong white bread flour

4 extra large eggs

Ingredients

3 extra large egg yolks

¾ cup superfine sugar

¼ cup custard powder or instant vanilla pudding

scant 1¾ cups whole milk

3 drops vanilla extract

scant ½ teaspoon fine salt

2 sticks unsalted butter at room temperature, cubed

But think positive! While the sugar is caramelizing, warm the milk in a separate pan over low heat. When the caramel is ready, add the milk very carefully, stirring gently. As soon as you have a honey-colored liquid—think fake tan—add the vanilla extract and salt. Pour the hot liquid on to the egg yolk mixture, stir well, then pour it back into the pan and simmer until it thickens to a paste-like consistency. Cool to 160°F, then add the butter, and mix to a glossy paste.

Remove from the heat and pour the mixture into the prepared baking sheet (organization is key). Cover the pan and its contents with plastic wrap, making sure that the film is in contact with the mixture to lock in moisture, and prevent it from drying out. Leave to cool for up to 2 hours.

The White Glaze

Find a pan large enough to dip a whole éclair into. Put the fondant icing in the pan and warm gently until the icing melts to a runny consistency. Remove from the heat and leave to settle.

Styling Details

Take a choux pastry finger and poke a hole in the bottom with a skewer. Transfer the salted caramel cream to a plastic piping bag fitted with a straight nozzle, then pipe the cream through the hole into what will be your éclair to fill it.

When the choux pastries are all filled with cream, carefully hold each one upside down and dip the top side into the glaze. Don't submerge it—you only want the top glazed. Let any excess glaze run off, then be a chef and run your finger smoothly and quickly along the top. You need to do all the dipping fast before the icing cools and hardens. Place the éclairs on a serving plate with the glaze facing up, and while the icing is wet, decorate with the flowers. Repeat until you have a line-up of very pretty éclairs.

Ingredients

7 oz ready-made white fondant icing

red edible flowers, to decorate

NICHOLAS KIRKWOOD

The Pearl Pump
Sachertorte

" *Restyle the Sachertorte
with glossy chocolate miroir
and mini pearls.* "

MK

The Pearl Pump Sachertorte ᒪᒪ

This rich chocolate cake was invented by the Austrian Franz Sacher in Vienna in 1882, and it is one of the most famous Viennese culinary specialities. Like our high-heeled inspiration, this takes a classic and adds modern style to its polish.

MAKES 40–60, but even this won't seem enough

You will need: 12 x 8-inch cake pan / baking parchment / stand mixer or hand-held electric beaters / kitchen thermometer / wire rack / palette knife / rolling pin / piping bag or toothpick

The Chocolate Sponge and Jam Filling

Preheat the oven to 350°F/325°F fan. Grease a 12 x 8-inch cake pan and line with baking parchment.

Melt the chocolate, then set aside to cool. Sift the flour, cocoa powder, and baking soda together into a bowl and set aside. Beat the butter and confectioners' sugar until pale and fluffy, then add the egg yolks and vegetable oil and beat thoroughly. Now it's time to beat in the melted chocolate. Finally, fold in the flour mixture.

Whisk the egg whites and superfine sugar to soft peaks in a grease-free bowl, then fold into the cake mixture. Pour it all into the prepared pan, level the top and bake for 15 minutes, until risen. Remove from the oven and leave to cool for a few minutes, then remove the sponge from the pan and leave it to cool on a wire rack.

Now for a tricky stage. Place the cooled sponge on the work surface and use a serrated knife to cut it in half horizontally. We cut our cake into three layers, as shown in the picture on the next page, but if this is your first attempt you will probably find it easier to stick to two.

Separate the two halves and spread the jam on top of one half, then place the second half on top to make a sandwich. Press down gently to ensure they are well stuck together, then place the cake in the fridge to rest for 1 hour.

Ingredients

2 oz dark chocolate, broken into pieces

1 cup all-purpose flour

1 heaping tablespoon cocoa powder

scant ¼ teaspoon baking soda

generous ½ stick softened unsalted butter, plus extra for greasing

¼ cup confectioners' sugar

3 extra large egg yolks

¼ cup vegetable oil

4 extra large egg whites

5 tablespoons superfine sugar

⅓ cup raspberry jam

The Chocolate Miroir

Soak the gelatin. While it is softening, put 4½ fl oz water in a pan with the sugar and glucose and bring to a boil, then add the cocoa powder and stir well. Slowly pour in the cream, stirring continuously. Add the drained gelatin to the pan and stir to dissolve, then strain the mixture into a pitcher and put it in the fridge to cool to 95°F. When it has cooled, give it a stir to stop it setting on the bottom.

Ingredients

4 leaves of gelatin

1 cup superfine sugar

about 1 teaspoon liquid glucose

¾ cup cocoa powder, sifted

scant ¾ cup heavy cream

Styling Details

Once the sponge has rested, remove it from the fridge and cut it into ¾ x 2-inch rectangular pieces. You should end up with 40–45, with some excess. Place the pieces on a wire rack, well spaced out, and set the rack over a tray or a sheet of baking parchment. Remove the chocolate miroir mixture from the fridge, and carefully pour it over the sponge pieces so that each is evenly glazed, allowing the excess to run off. Leave to set for a few minutes, then carefully slip a palette knife underneath each cake, and transfer it to a serving plate.

To decorate your cake pieces, roll out the fondant icing thinly on a work surface dusted with confectioners' sugar and cut small pieces the same length as the short end of your cakes, and ¼ inch wide. Brush with egg white and sprinkle with gold glitter. Leave to dry for a few minutes, then stick silver balls on to the glittery strip with small dots of icing, using either a piping bag or a toothpick. Once the pearls are in place, position the strip carefully on the end of one cake piece. Repeat for the other cake pieces.

Ingredients

confectioners' sugar, for dusting

2 oz yellow ready-made fondant icing

1 egg white

edible gold glitter

small quantity of runny icing (made from confectioners' sugar mixed with water)

edible silver balls (4 or 5 per cake)

GIAMBATTISTA VALLI

—

The Strawberry
Sugar Spin Roll

" *This dress is sugary sweet, so
I knew it had to be pink glitter
sponge with a spun sugar crown.* "

MK

The Strawberry Sugar Spin Roll ᒧᒧᒧ

A jelly roll might not sound the most sophisticated of cakes, but add a strawberry shade and spun sugar to make the ultimate fashion fairy cake.

MAKES AT LEAST 10—it's tricky, so make enough to enjoy

You will need: 12 x 16-inch cake pan (a 12 x 12-inch pan is also fine; your sponge will be a little thicker) / baking parchment / stand mixer or hand-held electric beaters / wire rack / sugar thermometer / 2 chopsticks / old newspaper

The Jelly Roll

Preheat the oven to 350°F/325°F fan. Grease a 12 x 16-inch or 12 x 12-inch cake pan and line with baking parchment.

Sift the all-purpose flour and cornstarch together into a small bowl. Soften the marzipan, put it in a bowl with the butter, and beat until soft and fluffy. Gradually add the egg yolks and keep mixing until they are fully incorporated.

In a separate, grease-free bowl, whisk the egg whites and sugar to soft peaks. Fold them into the butter mixture, and add the red food coloring. Then it's time to fold in the flour and cornstarch. Spread the mixture evenly in the prepared pan and bake for 10–12 minutes, until risen and pinky-golden. Leave it to cool in the pan on a wire rack for 1 hour. It may seem a long time, but the cake must be properly cool before you roll it, so enjoy the pause before the next stage.

When the cake is cold, place a sheet of baking parchment on your work surface and carefully turn the pan on to it, cake side down. Lift off the pan and gently peel the top layer of parchment off the sponge. Now spread the strawberry jam on to the sponge and start to roll it up gently from the longest side. Think long thin roll, not short and chunky. You can use the baking parchment underneath to help lift and roll the sponge, and you may find it easier to trim off the edges. Take care not to let it break, and make sure you don't include the paper inside the roll!

Once it is completely rolled up, put it in the fridge for 30 minutes and relax. When the time is up, brush the roll with edible silver glitter. At The Berkeley, we mix the glitter with a little glucose syrup for a longer-lasting finish. Cut the roll into small slices, about 1½ inches long, and turn them on one side, so the swirl faces up.

Ingredients

¼ cup all-purpose flour

⅓ cup cornstarch

2¼ oz marzipan, cut into chunks

½ stick softened unsalted butter, plus extra for greasing

3 extra large eggs, separated

5½ tablespoons superfine sugar

15 drops red liquid food coloring

scant 1 cup smooth strawberry jam

edible silver glitter, to decorate

The Spun Sugar

Put the superfine sugar and ⅔ cup water into a pan and bring to a boil, stirring occasionally to help the sugar dissolve. When it boils, stop stirring and add the food coloring. Boil until the water evaporates completely and the mixture has reached 310–320°F—check with a sugar thermometer—leaving you with pink, lightly caramelized sugar.

Remove the pan from the heat and carefully dip the base of the pan in a bowl of cold water for 5 seconds. Be careful: don't allow any cold water into the boiled sugar.

Now to make your spindle. Secure two chopsticks to the work surface 2–4 inches apart, with most of each chopstick hanging over the edge. Place some newspaper on the floor below to catch any drips; this is going to be messy. Take a fork and dip it into the melted sugar, then drizzle it quickly back and forth over the chopsticks like a cat's cradle to make spun sugar like yarn as it dries, creating a cotton candy effect.

Styling Details

Once you have a mass of pink strands, gently remove them from the chopsticks and place them on your worktop. Cut the spun sugar into 1½-inch-long sections and pinch each at the bottom to create a fanned-out effect. Stick the pinched end of the spun sugar in to crown each roll, and serve with panache.

Ingredients

1¼ cups superfine sugar

25 drops red liquid food coloring

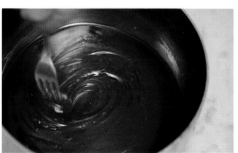

ZAC POSEN

———

The Vanilla & Chocolate
Spiral Heel Sponge

*" Stack these layers as high
as you dare if you love
high heels, chocolate, or both! "*

MK

The Vanilla & Chocolate Spiral Heel Sponge ∿

Attention to detail is a way to make a statement, so choose stripes in everyone's favorite flavors and they are bound to impress.

MAKES 7–10, depending on how high you go!

You will need: two 12 x 8-inch cake pans / baking parchment / stand mixer or hand-held electric beaters / wire rack / rolling pin / nonstick silicone mat / 1½-inch-diameter cookie cutter

The Chocolate Ribbon

You'll find it easiest to make these the day before and keep them in a cool place until you're ready to use them. Roll out the modeling chocolate to ¼ inch thick on a nonstick silicone mat. Using a sharp knife, cut out ¾ x 6¼-inch strips, one for each cake you are serving. Shape each strip into two loops and pinch them together, as shown opposite. If you're not sure about forming the loop, practice with a piece of paper or real ribbon first to get the shape. The chocolate will stick to itself through the heat from your hands, so no glue or bows are needed. Bend and stick, and when all the strips are done, leave them in a cool place until you're ready to assemble the total look.

Ingredients

* Make a day in advance *

3½ oz dark modeling chocolate

The Vanilla and Almond Sponge

Preheat the oven to 350°F/325°F fan. Grease a 12 x 8-inch cake pan and line with baking parchment.

Melt the butter, then leave to cool. Beat the ground almonds, confectioners' sugar, flour, and whole eggs for about 5 minutes, until pale and fluffy. Add the melted butter and vanilla extract and beat for another minute.

Now put the egg whites in a separate, grease-free bowl and whisk lightly with the superfine sugar until soft peaks form. Fold the whisked egg whites into the almond mixture, then it's ready to pour into the prepared pan. Bake for 15 minutes, until risen and golden, then leave to cool on a wire rack.

Ingredients

1 tablespoon butter, plus extra for greasing

heaping ¾ cup ground almonds

⅔ cup confectioners' sugar

2⅓ tablespoons all-purpose flour

2 extra large eggs

1 teaspoon vanilla extract

2 extra large egg whites

2½ teaspoons superfine sugar

The Chocolate Ganache

For part two of your stripe, line another 12 x 8-inch cake pan with baking parchment.

Melt the chocolate. Put the cream in a pan and bring it to a boil, then pour it gently over the melted chocolate. Stir well until it is silky smooth. Allow to cool for 30 minutes, then pour it into the prepared pan and spread it out evenly with a knife to make a layer about ¼ inch thick. Put it in the fridge to set for 2 hours.

Ingredients

10½ oz dark chocolate, broken into pieces

½ cup whipping cream

Styling Details

You need a steady, stylish hand to assemble your heel and add its character. When the vanilla and almond sponge and the chocolate ganache have set, use a 1½-inch-diameter cookie cutter to cut out circles from both. You should get about 20 from each pan. Stack them carefully in alternating layers, making sure the top disc is chocolate. Here we used three layers of each kind—but you can use even more, depending how high a heel you fancy, or how much cake you want. If you're having trouble sticking them together, fear not—as it comes to room temperature everything will stay where it should be! For real polish at The Berkeley, we brush the top layer with a sugar glaze to make it look extra glossy. Last but not least, place a chocolate ribbon on top of each cake heel to serve.

THE ROYAL COLLECTION

The Regal Red
Velvet Crown

*" It's complex to make
the crown jewels—but have
a try and crown yourself
queen of cakes. "*

MK

The Regal Red Velvet Crown ㅅㅅㅅ

To celebrate our longest-serving monarch, it seemed appropriate to create the ultimate challenge, from piped ermine to English apples and red velvet crowned with chocolate curves.

MAKES 12

You will need: blender / twelve 1¾-inch-diameter half-sphere silicone molds / shallow 9½-inch square cake pan / baking parchment / stand mixer or hand-held electric beaters / skewer / 1½-inch-diameter cookie cutter / kitchen thermometer / wire rack / paper piping bag / rolling pin

The Apple Domes
The apple domes can be made ahead and kept in the freezer. Spread this cake out over a few evenings and pace yourself.

First, make an apple purée: peel and core the apples, cut them into quarters and put them in a blender. Add 2½ teaspoons of the sugar and blend to a smooth purée.

Soak the gelatin. Put the apple purée in a pan with the remaining sugar and bring to a boil. Gradually add the eggs and the extra yolks, stirring continuously. Cook over low heat, still stirring, until the mixture starts to thicken. Add the drained gelatin to the mixture along with the pink food coloring and stir until everything has dissolved. Remove from the heat, transfer the mixture to a bowl, and leave it to cool for 30 minutes.

Once it has cooled, add the butter and beat well until it is completely incorporated. Pour the mixture into twelve 1¾-inch-diameter half-sphere silicone molds, and put them in the freezer for at least 2 hours.

The Chocolate Glaze
Melt the dark and milk chocolates together, then set aside to cool. Put the cream, stock syrup, and glucose in a pan and bring to a boil, then slowly pour it on to the melted chocolate and mix well. Finally, add the grapeseed oil, mix thoroughly and leave to cool for 30 minutes.

Ingredients

* Can be made in advance *

3 dessert apples

7½ tablespoons superfine sugar

2 leaves of gelatin

2 extra large eggs, plus two extra large egg yolks

6 drops pink liquid food coloring

⅓ cup softened unsalted butter, cut into cubes

Ingredients

2 oz dark chocolate, broken into pieces

5½ oz milk chocolate, broken into pieces

4½ fl oz whipping cream

2 tablespoons stock syrup (see page 111)

5 teaspoons liquid glucose

1½ teaspoons grapeseed oil

The Red Velvet Cake

Preheat the oven to 350°F/325°F fan. Grease and line a shallow 9½-inch square cake pan with baking parchment.

Sift the flour, cocoa powder, and baking soda together and set aside. Put the butter, sugar, salt, and vanilla in a bowl and beat until pale and fluffy. Gradually add the egg, mix well, then add the flour and cocoa mixture. Still gently beating, add the buttermilk slowly, then the white wine vinegar, and don't forget the food coloring. Mix well.

Pour the mixture into the prepared pan and bake for about 20 minutes, until a skewer inserted into the center comes out clean. Take the cake out of the oven and leave to cool for 30 minutes. Cut out twelve 1½-inch-diameter circles with a cookie cutter and set them aside. You should have some leftover cake; this can be frozen for the next party or coronation tea-time treat!

Ingredients

1 cup minus 1 tablespoon all-purpose flour

scant 2 tablespoons cocoa powder

1 teaspoon baking soda

½ stick softened unsalted butter, plus extra for greasing

¾ cup superfine sugar

a pinch of salt

1 teaspoon vanilla extract

1 extra large egg

½ cup buttermilk

1 teaspoon white wine vinegar

20 drops red liquid food coloring

The Cake Coronation

First check the temperature of your chocolate glaze; if it's cooler than 95°F, reheat it very gently so that it's easy to pour. Carefully unmold the apple domes and place them on the red velvet sponge circles. Space the cakes out on a wire rack set over a tray or sheet of baking parchment, and pour the chocolate glaze over to cover entirely, allowing the excess to run off. Let the glaze set for about 5 minutes, then carefully remove the cakes from the rack, and transfer them to a serving plate to decorate.

To make the icing, mix the confectioners' sugar and egg white to the consistency of lip gloss, then add the red food coloring and stir well—or feel free to cheat by using ready-made red icing! Put the icing in a small paper piping bag and cut off the tip to make a small hole. This is your glue for sticking the decorations in place.

On a work surface lightly dusted with confectioners' sugar, roll out the fondant icing to ⅛ inch thick. Cut a ¼ x 5 inch strip and place it around the base of one crown to check the fit, then use this piece as a guide to cut strips for all 12 crowns. Add dots of red icing all around to make the "ermine."

Roll out the modeling chocolate on a nonstick flat surface to a thickness of ⅛ inch and cover lightly with edible glitter. Cut out 60 squares measuring ⅜ x ⅜ inch, five per crown, and score a diagonal cross in each. Pipe a dot of red icing on to the center of each square to make the "jewels." (We also made some green icing to decorate one square for the topmost jewel on the crown.) Stick four squares evenly spaced around the base of each crown, as shown; you will have 12 left over for later.

For the distinctive arch—you're nearly there!—cut 48 strips measuring ¼ x 2¾ inches from the modeling chocolate, to give four per crown. Bend each strip slightly to make a neat curve. Using the red icing as glue, attach four curves to each cake, starting at the top of each square gem and finishing at the center of the top of the crown. You may find it helps to make these a few hours in advance so that they have time to dry.

Roll tiny pieces of modeling chocolate into small balls, roughly ¼ inch in diameter, and place one at the center point of the top of each crown. Place one leftover ⅜-inch square on top of each ball, again using icing to secure it. If you've made it this far, you truly are a baking queen!

Ingredients

heaping ⅓ cup confectioners' sugar, plus extra for dusting

1 extra large egg white

5 drops red liquid food coloring

2 oz ready-made white fondant icing

7 oz ready-made pale brown modeling chocolate

edible glitter spray, to decorate

The Designer Cookie Collection

Take this classic dough recipe and transform the cookie into the designer number you can't resist. Keep your sweet tooth on trend using the recipe below and let the following pages inspire your own fully fashioned designer cookie collection.

MAKES 10–12

You will need: stand mixer or hand-held electric beaters / plastic wrap rolling pin / 2 baking sheets / baking parchment / wire rack / paper piping bags

Ingredients

5 tablespoons unsalted butter, softened

heaping ⅓ cup superfine sugar

1 extra large egg

scant 1¼ cups all-purpose flour, sifted, plus extra for dusting

You can choose one of the following flavorings for extra spice or style

1 vanilla bean, split lengthwise and seeds scraped out

2 teaspoons ground ginger

⅓ cup poppy seeds

finely grated zest of 2 lemons

scant 2 tablespoons cocoa powder (for this variation, use a heaping 1 cup all-purpose flour in the dough recipe)

The Cookie Dough

Beat the butter and sugar until pale and fluffy. Add the egg and your chosen flavoring at this stage, then beat for another minute. Quickly mix in the flour, but stop beating as soon as it has combined, to avoid over-mixing it. Wrap the dough in plastic wrap and put it in the fridge to rest for 1½ hours. Meanwhile, prepare your designer template—boot, bikini, coat, or shoe—by tracing the shape from the back of the book on to a plastic lid and cutting it out.

Once the dough has rested, take it out of the fridge and knead it gently. Dust your work surface and rolling pin with flour, and roll the dough out to a thickness of ¼ inch.

Tip: If you find the dough a bit sticky, try sandwiching it between two sheets of baking parchment and rolling that instead.

Transfer the rolled-out dough carefully to a baking sheet (your rolling pin should help here), and return it to the fridge for another 30 minutes.

Preheat the oven to 350°F/325°F fan. Line a baking sheet with baking parchment. Take the chilled dough out of the fridge and place the template you have made on top. Carefully cut around it with a small, sharp knife to create your collection of mini pieces. Place the cut cookie shapes on the prepared baking sheet and bake for just 8 minutes, until pale brown around the edges. Remove from the oven and leave to cool on a wire rack for 20 minutes.

The Designer Top Coat

The Outline Icing

Whisk the egg white into the confectioners' sugar a little at a time to create a smooth paste the consistency of lip gloss. Add food coloring to get the shade you want, depending on the cookie you are making.

Ingredients

1½ cups confectioners' sugar

1 extra large egg white

5 drops liquid food coloring

The Filling Icing

Whisk the egg whites into the confectioners' sugar a little at a time to create a runny liquid. Filling icing needs to be a little runnier than outline icing—think nail varnish—hence the extra egg white. Add food coloring again to get the shade you want, depending on the cookie you are making.

Ingredients

1½ cups confectioners' sugar

2 extra large egg whites

5 drops liquid food coloring

Icing the Cookies

Fill a small piping bag no more than two-thirds full with the outline icing and cut the tip off to create a very small hole. Whatever shape you are styling, it's the same process. First carefully pipe a line all the way around the edge of the cooled baked cookie to create the outline, along with any other necessary line details. Follow the photographs for each designer to guide you on the details of each design. Leave to set for a few minutes.

Once the outline has set, fill another piping bag with the filling icing. Cut a slightly larger hole in the tip this time and "flood" the central part of the cookie with icing until it reaches the outline (see right). You can pick up and gently tilt the cookie to help the icing to spread, if necessary. Leave it to dry completely, at least 1 hour, before you start working on the details, again following the photographs of the design or the original if you have it.

Icing Tips

Holding the piping bag with both hands can make it easier to control the line you are icing. Hold the bag straight and vertical above the surface you are piping on to, but not too close to it, and squeeze from the top, applying an even pressure. Try to move it fairly quickly to get an even line. It's a good idea to practice on a piece of baking parchment before committing to the cookie.

Your piped outline will dry quickly. By the time you have piped an outline on ten cookies, the first should be ready for flooding.

MANOLO BLAHNIK

—

The Blahnik
Cookie

" *Who doesn't love shoes?*
Spice it up with a touch of
ginger and edible sparkle. "

MK

The Blahnik Cookie ⌐⌐

*The Hangisi is one of Manolo's most iconic shoes,
so why not make a rainbow of options—you can
never have enough of his high heels.*

Ingredients

classic cookie dough
(see page 78), flavored with
2 teaspoons ground ginger—
Manolo's favorite

outline and filling icing in
colors of your choice for
the shoe and insole

silver glitter or decorations
of your choice

**Template at the
back of the book**

Prepare the dough, make your high heel
template, then cut out and bake the cookies.

Template Tips

Place the template on the dough and use the tip of a knife
to cut around the template. When you have gone all the way
around, slip the knife underneath to help lift it from the
dough. Keep cutting shapes until you have enough of a
collection, re-rolling the leftover dough until it is all used up.
If you have a marble slab, roll your cookie dough out on that,
as it will help to keep the dough cool.

To ice, decide on your color scheme, using the picture or making
this an excuse to purchase the real thing for inspiration. First
pipe the outline of the shoe in your preferred color, then pipe the
outline of the insole, following the picture. Next carefully flood
in the shoe color, matching your outline, followed by the nude
color for the insole.

When the shoe is dry, use your outline icing to go around the
edge again in the shoe color to emphasize the sole and arch
of the heel.

To create the iconic tip on the toe of each shoe, we used white
icing mixed with edible silver glitter, but you could use ready-
made decorations such as silver balls instead. Finally, add a
contrasting heel tip using your nude tone to finish.

BURBERRY

—

The Tea Trench
Cookie

*"You can't guarantee the
weather, so polish your piping
skills by icing up a tea–time
trench come rain or shine."*

MK

The Tea
Trench Cookie ⌐⌐

*Guests staying at The Berkeley will find a
Burberry trench in their room—but even if you
aren't lucky enough to be staying at the hotel,
you can wear an apron and ice a trench with this
delicious cookie that mixes tradition with trend.*

Prepare the dough, cut out your regiment of trenches
and bake the cookies. Once out of the oven and cooled,
they are ready to ice.

First pipe the outline of the trench, following the
photographs, then flood with the main coat color icing.

Leave to dry, then add the outlines of collar and lapels,
trying to keep all your work uniform. Finally, add the
contrasting details such as the belt tie and cuffs, allow
to set, and you're ready to serve.

Ingredients

classic cookie dough
(see page 78), flavored with
⅓ cup poppy seeds

outline and filling icing in
trench tones of your choice

black or dark brown icing
for detailing

**Templates at the
back of the book**

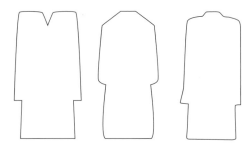

HEIDI KLEIN

The Bikini
Cookie

*" What could say summer
more than this? Every year we
do a bikini cookie. Ice on her
belly button and leave her to
sunbathe on your saucer. "*

MK

The Bikini Cookie ⌐⌐⌐

Choose your bikini and sun-factor shading and get ready to ice. Add a touch of vanilla, and you can even try a gluten- or wheat-free version while thinking about your figure.

Ingredients

classic cookie dough (see page 78), flavored with 1 vanilla bean, split lengthwise and seeds scraped out

skin-colored icing for outlining and flooding

icing for the bikini, the color is up to you

alternative icing color for detailing (depending on pattern or style)

fine black edible icing pen (for the belly button!)

Prepare the dough, cut out your sunbathing silhouette and bake the cookies. Once cool, you can ice them.

Choose your tan tone and first outline the entire body shape, then flood to fill.

Leave to set. Next pipe the outline of your bikini—or swimsuit, for a touch of modesty—in your chosen colors.

Use the same icing to fill, cutting the tip of your piping bag fractionally bigger, to release more icing, but still give you enough control to fill a small area.

We finished our cookies with little yellow dots to imitate the gold trim on the bikini, but pattern or finish yours as you wish.

One important final touch is the belly button: at The Berkeley we use an icing pen, but you could use a drop of icing instead. Just don't forget it!

Template at the back of the book

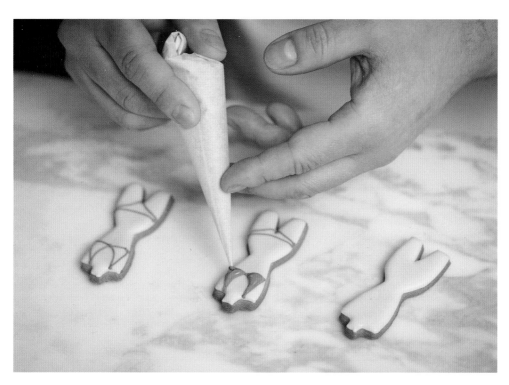

CHARLOTTE OLYMPIA

—

The Bootie
Cookie

*" This two-tone bootie
design is simple, yet
attention-grabbing. "*

MK

The Bootie Cookie ⌐⌐⌐

This cookie design was created exclusively for this book. Charlotte Olympia's boots have been a very popular cookie throughout Prêt-à-Portea's history, so we wanted to create an advanced version of our chocolate classic.

Ingredients

classic cookie dough (see page 78), made with a heaping 1 cup all-purpose flour and flavored with scant 2 tablespoons cocoa powder

red and black icing, enough for outlining, flooding, and detailing

Template at the back of the book

Prepare the dough, making the chocolate version or staying classic if you prefer, then cut out your booties and bake the cookies. To ice, once cool, first pipe a thin red outline for the upper arch zigzag, following the shape in the photograph opposite. Leave to dry for a few minutes before flooding this upper section with red icing. Leave to dry again, then pipe a black line as shown, and leave to dry before flooding the area with black icing. Once all this has set, pipe a red heel, and add a small black heel tip to complete the striking bootie.

How to Make a Paper Piping Bag

Piping bags and nozzles are widely available, but you can make your own from baking parchment.

This is how it's done at The Berkeley, and it's also useful when you need to pipe small amounts in different colors.

Starting with a large triangle of baking parchment, hold on to one corner with your thumb and wrap the other corner around to meet it, keeping the point sharp, to make a cone as shown in the photographs opposite.

Fold down one of the sticking-up corners to secure the bag, or you can secure it with a small piece of sticky tape on the outside.

Fill the bag two-thirds full with icing, then snip off the point with scissors to make a very small hole.

Use immediately.

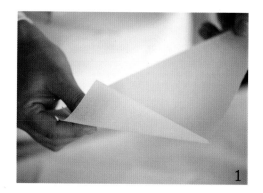

DIANE VON FURSTENBERG

The Gold Wrap
Cookie

*" Celebrate the female form
and serve this iconic dress
as glitter cookies! "*

MK

The Gold Wrap Cookie ∿∿

These elegant cookies were created to commemorate the 40th anniversary of DVF's iconic wrap dress. They are sprinkled with gold glitter and flavored with a delicious surprise note of lemon.

Ingredients

classic cookie dough (see page 78), flavored with the finely grated zest of 2 lemons

dark yellow icing for outlining and flooding

edible gold glitter

skin-colored icing for flooding

paler yellow icing for detailing

Template at the back of the book

Prepare the dough, roll it out, cut out your DVF silhouette, and bake the cookies. Leave to cool.

When you're ready to ice them, first pipe the outline of the dress with the darker yellow icing, following the photographs—remember to pipe an outline for the leg to peep through!

Leave to dry for a few minutes, then flood the same color icing within this outline to complete the dress shape. DVF is known for her prints, but this iconic wrap was all gold, so tap edible gold glitter over the iced dress and leave to dry.

Next, fill in the leg area with skin-colored icing.

When this is dry, it's as though you're adding the final accessories to a look: pipe the waistline, neckline, and around the leg with the paler yellow icing and get the party started.

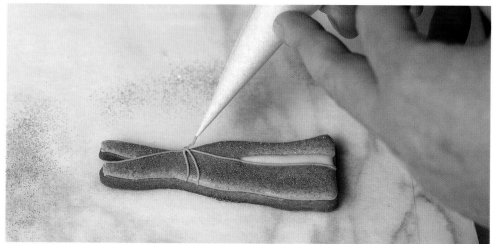

CHRISTIAN LOUBOUTIN

—

The Red Sole & Sparkle
Cookie

*" Everyone recognizes this flash
of red, so why not ice your own
iconic sole selection? "*

MK

The Red Sole & Sparkle Cookie ᴗᴗ

Here's a chance to have as many shoes as you can eat, and ice … This stiletto heel is also great for showing off your "cracking" technique to mirror the glittering effect of this silver pump.

Ingredients

classic cookie dough (see page 78), flavored as you like—or why not keep it buttery and classic?

white icing for outlining and flooding

edible silver glitter

red and black icing for detailing

Template at the back of the book

Prepare the dough, cut out lots of high heels, and bake the cookies.

To ice your shoe collection, first pipe the outline of the shoe in white, leaving an area of the shoe bare, as in the photograph. Now flood inside your outline with white icing.

Leave this to set for 2 minutes, then gently "poke" the surface all over with a toothpick or a clean fork.

Now dip a small brush in silver glitter and tap it all over the icing before it has fully set, without letting the brush touch the icing. The dimpled surface will set off the glitter and highlight the effect.

When the icing has set, you need a steady hand to apply that all-important line of red to the sole.

Do a few test lines on baking parchment first, or practice on the template to get the shape and thickness right.

For best results, keep the bag quite high above the cookie, and gently drag the line of icing where you want it to go. This makes it easier to produce a smooth line and also to follow the shape of the sole.

Finally, pipe the black heel tip on each cookie.

Leave to set, and these shoes are made for walking, and serving with tea.

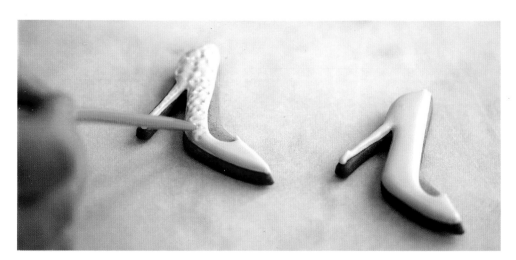

Techniques & Tips

Whether you are a "shoe chef" or a choux pastry chef, for all those aspiring Marie Antoinettes, here are some tips to help you navigate the skilled world of patisserie.

Bavarois
This classic French dessert is made from flavored pastry cream (crème pâtissière) set with *gelatin.*

Chocolate: see *Melting chocolate; Modeling chocolate*

Choux pastry
This light, fluffy, twice-cooked pastry is most famously used for cream puffs and éclairs. It can be spooned or piped into shape and is often filled with cream.

Compote
Quick and simple to make, compote is a mixture of fruit, sugar, and a little water, cooked until thickened and syrupy, sometimes with spices.

Creaming ingredients
Creaming involves mixing two ingredients, usually butter and sugar, until they form a light, pale, smooth mixture with no lumps. A wooden spoon and plenty of elbow grease will do the job, but hand-held electric beaters or a *stand mixer* will make it much easier.

Cutting cake portions
To ensure a neat finish for small cake pieces, trim the large cake before you start, so that you'll have smooth edges to work with.

Delice
A layered confection of different flavors and textures. A delice can be made of a variety of elements including sponge, or cookie with mousse and meringue.

Eggs
All eggs used in these recipes are extra large. You can buy liquid egg white in the chilled section of the supermarket. One extra large egg white weighs about 1⅓ oz. To separate an egg, break it carefully on the edge of a cup or small bowl and pass the yolk from one half of the shell to the other until as much of the white as possible has dropped into the cup. It's a fiddly job, but gets easier with practice. The most important thing is to make sure that none of the yolk ends up in the white. Leftover yolks from the recipes in this book can be used to make custard, mayonnaise, or certain types of pastry; spare whites are perfect for meringues and macaroons.

Excess baggage
Any leftover cake (not iced or decorated) can be wrapped well and frozen. Extra icing (for example if you have poured icing over cakes standing on a rack set over a tray) can be stored in the fridge. To re-use it, allow it to come to room temperature and stir well. Any mousse that doesn't fit in your shot glasses can be poured into ramekins or bowls, and kept in the fridge for dessert.

Folding ingredients
Folding is a way of combining two mixtures without over-mixing or knocking out too much air. Cut through the mixture using a metal spoon or a spatula and fold it over repeatedly in a figure-eight motion until it is just combined; avoid stirring.

Fondant icing (ready-made)
Semi-hard fondant icing is sold in blocks, which can be rolled out and used to decorate cakes, cookies and other confections. It's available in a variety of colors, but if you can't find the color you want, buy white and knead in *food coloring.*

Fondant icing sugar
This icing sugar with added glucose creates a soft, glossy icing that does not set hard.

Food coloring
Liquid food coloring is available in most supermarkets in a limited range of colors; online suppliers and specialist baking shops sell a wider range of colors in liquid, gel, or paste form. Gel or paste food colors are useful because they

are very concentrated and do not make the icing too runny; they are also easier to use with ready-made *fondant icing*. Use a toothpick to add a very small amount to the icing, then stir or knead it through until the color is even.

Ganache
Used as a filling, icing, sauce, or glaze for pastries and cakes, ganache is made by pouring hot cream over chopped chocolate, and stirring to combine. It has a lighter texture than pure melted chocolate, and a softer set.

Gelatin
This setting agent derived from animal collagen is available in powdered or leaf form. To use leaf gelatin, fully immerse the sheets in cold water for 5 minutes, or until they are very floppy, but have not disintegrated. Drain them, add to a warm mixture as instructed in the recipe, and stir to dissolve. Be careful not to boil a mixture that has had gelatin added to it. Vegetarian alternatives, such as agar agar, are available but they tend to give a firmer set. Always follow the directions on the package carefully. Gelatin leaves usually weigh 0.07–0.1 oz; in this book we have assumed 0.1 oz per leaf.

Gianduja
A sweet paste made from chocolate and hazelnuts; a more easily available, if slightly less refined equivalent is Nutella.

Grease-free bowl
When whisking egg whites, it's crucial that your bowl is scrupulously clean, since any grease will stop the whites from thickening. To make sure your bowl is clean enough, rub the inside with the cut edge of half a lemon.

Kitchen thermometer
This thermometer has a lower range than a sugar thermometer, and is useful for checking that mousses or hot liquids have cooled to the correct temperature.

Liquid glucose
This liquid sugar syrup has a variety of uses, and is available from larger supermarkets and baking shops. Adding it to icing gives shine, and makes the result softer.

Measuring honey
Honey can be tricky to measure accurately. A useful technique is to use a metal spoon that has been heated in boiling water for a few moments, or to grease the spoon and weighing bowl lightly with oil.

Medium peaks: see *Whisking*

Melting chocolate
When melting chocolate, take care not to let it get too hot, or it may "seize" and turn thick and grainy. Break it into small pieces, place it in a heatproof bowl, and sit the bowl over a pan of hot water that is just simmering, not boiling. Make sure the base of the bowl does not touch the water. Turn off the heat under the pan and let the chocolate sit until it has melted, stirring it occasionally. Try to resist the delicious aroma!

Miroir
This classic French dessert is usually made up of a delicate sponge and mousse with a flat, shiny glaze on top. The word can also refer to the glaze itself.

Modeling chocolate
Glucose syrup and vegetable oil are added to chocolate to make a moldable paste that can be used to create shapes out of chocolate. It is available online and from specialist baking shops; it is also possible to make your own at home.

Nonstick silicone mat
This reusable, ovenproof, flexible mat is coated with silicone, which prevents foods from sticking. It can be used to line baking sheets for baking, or as a nonstick surface for rolling out.

Panna cotta
Literally "cooked cream," this classic Italian dessert of sweetened and sometimes flavored cream is set with gelatin.

Praline
This confection of almonds or hazelnuts, sugar, and sometimes cream is brittle and crunchy in France and softer in America. The word can also simply be used for a mixture, pastry, cake, or dessert that contains nuts.

Rolling out
Use a clean work surface, marble board, or *nonstick silicone mat* and a rolling pin to roll out modeling chocolate and icing. If you're working with sugar paste or fondant icing, dust the surface and your rolling pin with cornstarch; if you're

rolling chocolate, dust with confectioners' sugar.

Separating eggs: see *Eggs*

Silicone molds

Flexible, heatproof silicone molds are used for baking and making confectionery. They are available in many shapes and sizes from kitchen stores and online.

Soft peaks: see *Whisking*

Softening butter

Butter should be soft before you cream it or mix it into a cake or cookie batter. To do this, remove it from the fridge the night before baking. If you forget, you can cut the cold butter into large chunks and place it in a bowl of lukewarm water for 10 minutes, then drain off the water thoroughly.

Softening marzipan

The simplest way to soften marzipan is to knead it vigorously with your hands on a work surface. Kneading in a little water or a drop of vanilla or almond extract will also help. If you have a microwave, 1 minute at medium power and then a gentle knead will have the same effect. Alternatively, if you plan ahead, you can leave it in an airtight container with a few slices of orange for one or two days, but make sure the orange doesn't touch the marzipan.

Spun sugar

This most ethereal and sophisticated of decorations is made using hot, caramelized sugar, which is spun and flicked to create thin strands that become crunchy when set.

Stand mixer

This large electric food mixer has a removable bowl and different attachments for mixing, whisking, and kneading.

Stiff peaks: see *Whisking*

Stock syrup

This very simple syrup is made from water and sugar. To make it, place 1 cup sugar in a pan with a scant cup of water and heat gently, stirring, until the sugar has dissolved completely. Allow to cool, then store in a sealed container in the fridge.

Sugar paste

A stiff paste made from sugar, this can be rolled out and cut to make intricate decorative designs such as flowers. It dries out completely and becomes fragile. It's available online and from specialized baking stores.

Sugar thermometer

This thermometer is designed to be immersed in boiling sugary liquids at very high temperatures. Sugar syrups have different properties according to temperature, so it is important to watch them carefully. If you do not have a thermometer, when making a caramel, keep a close eye on the pan and take it off the heat as soon as the edge of the syrup starts to turn dark brown. Swirl the pan gently to distribute the dark color, and the syrup should take on a uniform golden-brown color. Return the pan to the heat to cook for a few seconds longer if it's not quite there. Always take extreme care when working with hot sugar.

Tablespoons/teaspoons

All spoon measurements given in this book are level. The easiest way to get a level measurement is to fill the spoon with the ingredient and carefully skim off the top with a knife or your finger.

Templates

The templates in this book are all given at actual size. The easiest way to use them for cutting out cookies is to trace the design on to parchment or tracing paper, transfer the outline to a spare plastic lid, and cut it out.

Tuile

A tuile (French for "tile") is a thin, delicate cookie made from a batter that is malleable right after baking. Tuiles can be rolled around spoon handles or otherwise molded, or baked flat and layered with cream and fruit; once cooled they set firm.

Whisking: soft/medium/stiff peaks

These terms describe how stiff whisked egg whites or whipped cream should be. For soft peaks, the mixture should just about hold a peak when you remove the whisk, but the peak will sag. For medium peaks, it should be slightly stiffer, and only the very tip of the peak will sag. For stiff peaks, the peaks should hold their own weight, and point upwards. Take care and proceed with caution, as these stages can be reached quickly, and cream continues to thicken after you stop whisking.

The Berkeley would like to add special thanks to Paula Fitzherbert, John Small, Frances Asta, Simon Neggers, Christina Norton, Olivia Johnson, Orla Hickey, Eliza Fitzherbert, Eunmi Jung, John Carey, Mourad Khiat, and his brilliant pastry team at the hotel. Particular thanks to Camilla Morton for her continued support and love for this book and all at Laurence King Publishing for bringing this book to life.

To all those past and present who have inspired and enjoyed Prêt-à-Portea, this book is for you.

The Berkeley,
Wilton Place,
London
SW1X 7RL

the-berkeley.co.uk
0207 235 6000

First published in 2016
by Laurence King Publishing Ltd
361–373 City Road
London EC1V 1LR
Tel: +44 20 7841 6900
Fax: +44 20 7841 6910
email: enquiries@laurenceking.com
www.laurenceking.com

This book was designed and produced by Laurence King Publishing Ltd, London.

A catalogue record for this book is available from the British Library

ISBN: 978 1 78067 872 6

Recipes by Mourad Khiat

Printed in China

Picture credits
All photography © John Carey except the following: pp9, 17, 31, 35, 45, 49, 65, 91 Catwalking; p13 courtesy Anya Hindmarch; pp23, 73 Getty; p27 courtesy Jimmy Choo; p41 courtesy Paul Smith; p55 courtesy Simone Rocha; p59 courtesy Nicholas Kirkwood; p69 FIRSTVIEW; p79 courtesy Manolo Blahnik; p83 courtesy Burberry; p87 courtesy Christian Louboutin; p95 courtesy Charlotte Olympia, Fall 2013 Hazel Boot from Once Upon a Time collection; p99 courtesy Heidi Klein; pp106, 109, 110 courtesy The Berkeley.